GLOBAL CULTU

American Indian Cultures

Ann Weil and Charlotte Guillain

Heinemann
LIBRARY
Chicago, Illinois

www.capstonepub.com
Visit our website to find out more information about Heinemann-Raintree books.

To order:
☎ Phone 800-747-4992
📖 Visit www.capstonepub.com to browse our catalog and order online.

Edited by Charlotte Guillain, Abby Colich, and Vaarunika Dharmapala
Designed by Steve Mead
Original illustrations © Capstone Global Library Ltd 2013
Illustrations by Oxford Designers & Illustrators
Picture research by Ruth Blair

Originated by Capstone Global Library Ltd
Printed and bound in China by Leo Paper Products Ltd

16 15 14 13 12
10 9 8 7 6 5 4 3 2 1

Library of Congress Cataloging-in-Publication Data
Weil, Ann.
  American Indian cultures / Ann Weil and Charlotte Guillain.
    p. cm.—(Global cultures)
  Includes bibliographical references and index.
  ISBN 978-1-4329-6781-9 (hb)—ISBN 978-1-4329-6790-1 (pb) 1. Indians of North America—History. 2. Indians of North America—Social life and customs. I. Guillain, Charlotte. II. Title.
  E77.W419 2013
  970.004'97—dc23   2011037705

Acknowledgments
We would like to thank the following for permission to reproduce photographs: Alamy pp. 5 (© Chuck Place), 14 (© Nancy G. Western Photography, Nancy Greifenhagen), 19 (© Pat Canova), 22 (© Mike Dobel), 27 (© Anders Ryman), 31 (© Buddy Mays), 35 (© Ralph William), 37 (© Trinity Mirror/Mirrorpix), 41 (© David R. Frazier Photolibrary, Inc.); Corbis pp. 9 (© Peter Turnley), 11 (© Werner Forman), 12 (© Nathan Benn), 16 (© Maggie Steber/National Geographic Society), 18 (© Kerrick James), 20 (© Marilyn Angel Wynn/Nativestock Pictures), 23 (© Boomer Jerritt/All Canada Photos), 26 (© Bettmann), 30 (© Christopher Felver), 32 (© Marilyn Angel Wynn/Nativestock Pictures), 38 (© George H. H. Huey), 40 (© Danny Lehman); Dreamstime.com design features (© Aroas); Getty Images pp. 6 (Paul Chesley), 10 (National Geographic/Willard R. Culver); Photoshot pp. 7, 15, 17, 29 (© UPPA), 34 (© EPA), 36 (© WpN); Shutterstock pp. 8 (© Jim Feliciano), 13 (© Tomaz Kunst), 24 (© Dennis Donohue), 33 (© Alan C. Heison), 43 top left (© pr2is), 43 bottom left (© Doug James), 43 top right (© Steffen Foerster Photography), 43 bottom right (© J. L. Levy).

Cover photograph of a smiling American Indian boy reproduced with permission of Alamy (© John Cancalosi). Cover design feature of a colorful textile reproduced with permission of Dreamstime.com (© Aroas).

CONTENTS

Introducing American Indian Cultures 4

Family and Society..............................6

Ornament 14

Beliefs and Ceremony 20

Daily Life and Customs 28

Performance...................................34

American Indian Cultures in the 21st Century 40

Timeline 42

Cultural Map......................................43

Glossary..44

Find Out More 46

Index 48

Some words are shown in bold, **like this**. You can find out what they mean by looking in the glossary.

INTRODUCING AMERICAN INDIAN CULTURES

What do you know about American Indians? Perhaps you have seen a totem pole or a Navajo rug. Perhaps you have heard of certain groups, such as the Cherokee, Sioux, or Apache.

American Indians are an important part of the history and **culture** of the United States. They lived here long before Europeans invaded, settled, and developed their own flourishing societies in North America. From the mid-1800s, the U.S. government forced many American Indians to live on **reservations**. Today, some choose to remain on reservations, while others live in towns and cities across the country.

Did you know?

There are over 500 American Indian tribes in the United States, and American Indians make up 1.5 percent of the population. The largest tribal groups include the Apache, Cherokee, Chippewa, Choctaw, Lumbee, Navajo, Pueblo, and Sioux.

What is culture?

Culture includes the values, beliefs, and attitudes of a particular place and people. It is about how people live and worship and about the music, art, and literature they produce. American Indians have never thought of themselves as one people with one culture. Each tribe or group developed its own beliefs, **customs**, languages, clothing, and homes over thousands of years.

This dancer from Tucson, Arizona, is wearing his **traditional** clothes for a special celebration.

FAMILY AND SOCIETY

In different American Indian cultures, families and communities work and live together in different ways. For example, the Blackfeet in the northern Plains traditionally lived in a band made up of 80 to 240 people, living in 10 to 30 **lodges**. Each band had a leader who was chosen by the group.

In the southeastern Cherokee culture, there are seven **clans**. Children become a member of their mother's clan. The Iroquois Confederacy is made up of six closely related tribes with nine clans. Although modern life has affected the way many American Indians live, people still have a very strong connection to their tribe or nation.

These Blackfeet children live in Montana. The Blackfeet are known to be brave warriors and excellent hunters.

Men's roles

Traditionally, American Indian men were warriors, **diplomats**, and hunters. Their main role was to protect, heal, and provide for their community. Men were also religious leaders. They led ceremonies to keep the people in harmony with natural and **spiritual** forces.

Plains Indians, such as the Cheyenne and Pawnee, depended on buffalo for food, clothes, and other necessities. Men tracked and killed the buffalo. Plains Indians also used horses, which had been introduced by the Spanish. Horses meant that people could travel over greater distances more easily.

This Navajo boy is holding a coup stick made of cactus wood.

Men also rode into battle. A warrior's importance depended on his skill and bravery. The bravest among the warriors carried **coup** sticks. If they touched an enemy with the stick, it was considered very brave. A notch was carved into the coup stick to record this bravery.

Women's roles

American Indian women have always gathered wild seeds, berries, and roots for food. They also look for herbs, which are used for healing. They know where to find these plants in the areas they live.

In most cultures, women were traditionally in charge of the home, taking care of babies and young children. Blackfeet women not only ran their homes, but they built them, too. When their community, or band, moved to new land, it was the women who carried the pieces of wood that made up their houses.

It is a woman's job to cut meat caught by the men into strips. Some is eaten fresh, but most is dried in the sun or cooked over a fire, to make it last longer. Plains Indians, such as the Arapaho and Sioux, make a food called pemmican by mixing pounded dried meat with fat and berries and then shaping it into cubes. In the past, pemmican was stored for use when **game** was scarce.

This is a *metate,* a stone instrument used by American Indian women for grinding corn or grain.

Women and leadership

Although American Indian leaders have traditionally been men, women have power, too. Among the Iroquois, women decide which men will be leaders. Northwest Coast women control how the tribe's money and land are used. In the Navajo culture, the women inherit their family's homes and rights to use land.

Wilma Pearl Mankiller (1945–2010)

Wilma Mankiller was the Cherokee Nation's first female principal chief. She held this office for 10 years, working hard to improve health and education for members of her tribe. She also built a strong relationship with the U.S. government and was awarded the Presidential Medal of Freedom in 1998.

Moving

After the European invasion, many American Indian tribes were forced to leave their traditional homelands. Others were forced to accept small reservations instead of the large areas of land they once occupied. Before this, many tribes had moved within their lands, following the herds of animals they hunted and finding fresh grazing land.

This Seminole man is carving a canoe from cypress wood.

American Indians took all their belongings when they moved, including their homes. Algonquin people carried loads on toboggans. These long sleds were made of thin, curved wood that moved quickly over snow. The Iroquois made long canoes that could hold more than 15 people. The Lenape in Delaware used sleds and snowshoes in winter, canoes on water, and pack dogs over land.

Tools and weapons

Traditionally, American Indians made their tools from materials such as bone, stone, wood, and plants. When Europeans arrived in the 1600s, Indians traded for objects they could not make themselves.

One of the most prized trade goods was the gun.

American Indian tribes sometimes went to war. Weapons included bow and arrows and axe-like tomahawks. Lenape warriors used war clubs and carried shields made of hide and wood. Some Indians used shields to protect themselves. Shields were decorated to make them powerful.

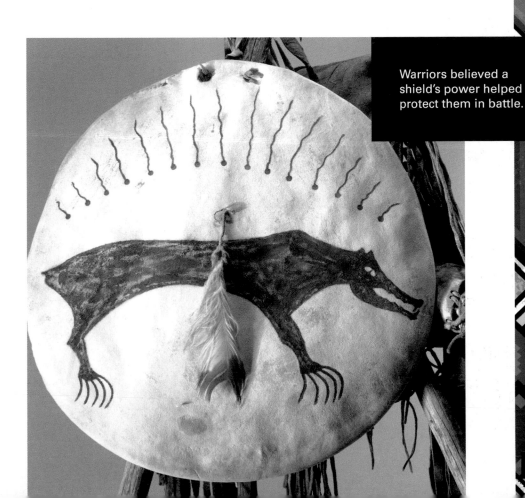

Warriors believed a shield's power helped protect them in battle.

11

Homes

Most American Indians live in modern houses today, but many also have traditional homes like their **ancestors** had. The Plains Indians, such as the Blackfeet, Comanche, and Cheyenne, traditionally lived in tent-like **tipis** covered in buffalo skins. The women took down and rebuilt the tipis when the group moved. Families today may take a tipi to festivals and gatherings.

Did you know?

Many people believe that all American Indians were **nomads** who lived in tipis. This image has been created by movies, television, and books. In fact, American Indians have many different traditional homes. All groups had their own settlements and moved to and from these throughout the year.

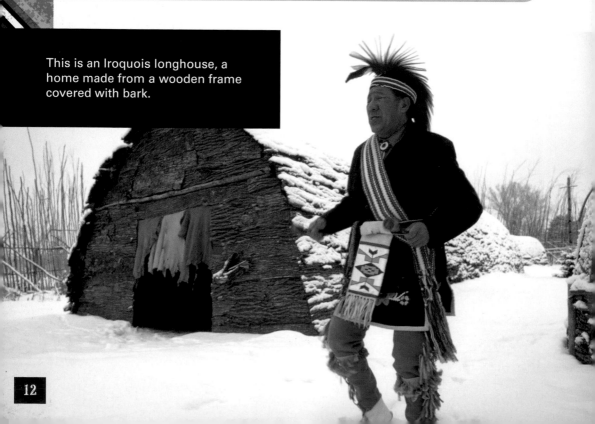

This is an Iroquois longhouse, a home made from a wooden frame covered with bark.

These Navajo *hogans* are in Monument Valley, Utah.

In other cultures, the type of home depended on the environment and local materials. The traditional Navajo dwelling in the Southwest was an eight-sided *hogan*. It was made from logs and mud with an earth roof. The Penobscot in the Northeast lived in small birchbark houses called wigwams.

Apaches lived in huts called *wickiups* made from arched poles covered with bark, grass, or branches. These structures were easy to take apart and carry from place to place. Northwest Coast Indians lived in sturdy plank houses, while the Seminoles in Florida lived in log cabins. After moving to swampy areas, they lived in structures called *chickees*, with floors raised up above the water.

ORNAMENT

Beauty is part of everything in American Indian life. Everyone creates beautiful objects, making items that people in a **Western** culture would call art.

Clothing

Today, most people, including American Indians, buy their clothes in stores. In the past, American Indians made everything they wore from materials they could find nearby or obtain through trade. Some American Indians were hunters who made clothes from animal skins. The Iroquois tribes hunted deer, so they made clothes from **tanned** buckskin. The Plains Indians, such as the Sioux and Blackfeet tribes, hunted buffalo and made warm robes from buffalo skins.

Some American Indians made clothes from plants woven together to make cloth. The Pueblo Indian tribes in the Southwest were farmers who made clothes from cotton.

Traditionally, many American Indian men wore a **breechcloth** and decorated leggings, such as these worn by a Sioux man.

Most American Indians today wear the same kinds of clothes as other Americans. Like most other cultures, many American Indians wear traditional styles of clothing for festivals, ceremonies, and other special occasions that celebrate their **heritage**.

Did you know?

Moccasins are soft leather shoes worn by many American Indian groups. Different tribes cut the leather and decorate their moccasins in different ways. The Ojibwe moccasins below are made from moosehide and decorated with beads.

The name Blackfeet is a translation of the word *siksika*. This described the dark moccasins the Blackfeet Indians wore.

Body paint

Many American Indian warriors painted their faces, bodies, and horses before going into battle. They believed this gave them protection. Others wore body paint for **rituals**. Each paint color had its own special meaning. Seminoles, for example, wore red paint during wartime and white paint during peacetime. When several tribes got together, each group could be identified by its body paint and clothing.

Today, American Indians, such as this Cherokee man, may wear face and body paint just as their ancestors did at celebrations and festivals.

Beadwork

American Indians use small shells, feathers, and porcupine quills to decorate clothes, moccasins, and other items. Some also make beads from materials such as precious stones found where they live. For example, tribes in the Southwest, such as the Navajo and Apache, use turquoise beads in their jewelry and decoration. Today, small glass beads are commonly used for decoration. These were introduced by Europeans about 500 years ago.

Each American Indian culture developed new patterns. Kiowa women owned the designs they created. This meant no one else could copy it without the owner's permission.

This Ojibwe bag is decorated with geometric patterns.

YOUNG PEOPLE

Some groups of American Indians, such as the Cheyenne, make beaded pouches, often in the shape of animals such as turtles. These are used to hold a piece of a baby's **umbilical cord** after he or she is born. The child can then keep the pouch for good luck.

Weaving

Members of the Coast Salish tribes on the Northwest Coast still wear blanket robes, as their ancestors did in the past. Traditionally, these blankets were woven from the hair of mountain goats.

Sheep were introduced to the Southwest by the Spanish about 400 years ago. The Navajo people began raising sheep for wool, which they used to weave blankets. These blankets have become famous for their beauty. The patterns often include brightly colored geometric shapes and zigzags. Weavers used light tools and often wove outside, where there was plenty of light and space to work.

Baskets were another woven household item. Many cultures, including the Pomos, Apaches, and Algonquins, used grasses and strips of tree bark to make baskets.

Today, most Navajo women learn how to weave.

Pottery

Many cultures use clay to make containers to hold food, water, and objects. American Indians in different regions used their local clay to make pottery. Groups in the Mississippi Valley made pots shaped like people. Other groups made coil pots, using long tubes of clay coiled into the shape of a container. Different cultures decorated pottery in various ways. For example, in the Southwest, the Mimbres people painted their pottery with animal designs, while the Mogollon culture used spiral patterns.

American Indians still make pots today, but now they are mostly sold to tourists and collectors or are used on special occasions.

Maria Montoya Martinez (1887–1980)

The Pueblo Indian Maria Montoya Martinez was an artist and potter who lived in New Mexico. She learned a traditional method of making coil pots and used ancient techniques to fire (bake) and glaze (cover in a shiny coating) her work. Her deep black pottery made her famous around the world.

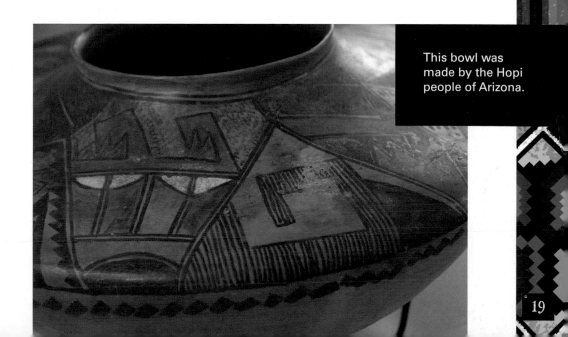

This bowl was made by the Hopi people of Arizona.

BELIEFS AND CEREMONY

American Indian cultures do not separate religion from everyday life the way people of other cultures do. Instead, they express their religion in almost everything they do. Traditionally, hunting was sacred, or holy. American Indians believed the animal **sacrificed** its body so the people could eat. They believe the land is sacred. Some Indian **creation stories** describe particular places. These stories tell how each group of people came to be on their land, along with the animals and plants that also live there.

Medicine wheels represent harmony and are used for rituals, healing, and teaching. They are always made up of white, yellow, red, and black stones.

For many American Indians, there are three stages in a person's life that have a strong spiritual significance: birth, becoming an adult, and death. Some tribes perform special rituals at the place where a baby is born. That place is then sacred to the person and remains important throughout his or her life. This spiritual connection to the land was one reason American Indians suffered so much when they were forced to live on reservations, sometimes away from their homelands.

Even war was sacred. When they went to war, warriors used special sacred words instead of speaking the way they would at home. Many believed their ancestors' spirits continued to live after their bodies had died.

Medicine bundles are an important part of Blackfeet Indians' spiritual life. These are bundles of items needed for a special ritual or ceremony, wrapped in cloth or hide. They could contain things like herbs, paint, clothing, or tools. The Blackfeet believe these bundles have power when used in particular rituals and special ceremonies, and they can be saved and passed on to someone else.

Did you know?

The spirit world is an important part of American Indian life. American Indians believe that all things, including animals, humans, and plants, have a spirit. People pray and carry out special rituals to connect with these spirits and try to achieve balance in their lives. Some rituals involve telling creation stories. It is considered important to show great respect for the natural world.

Totem poles

Northwest Coast peoples make totem poles. Totem poles are tall structures carved out of cedar wood. Many have images of animals, such as bears and birds, carved into the wood. The images often tell creation stories or describe the history of a powerful family. The poles were put in front of people's lodges and were often brightly painted. Today, skilled American Indian artists carve new poles for museums and collectors and teach the art to new generations.

Masks

In many American Indian cultures, masks are an important part of rituals and ceremonies. Northwest Coast Indians carve masks out of wood. The masks can show spirits, famous ancestors, or animals. People believe the tree sacrificed part of itself so the people could have the mask. They believe that just as a tree was alive, so is the mask. The masks are still worn when stories are told, and some have movable pieces to change the wearer's voice or expression.

The tallest totem poles can be almost 50 feet (15 meters) high.

The Navajo and Apache peoples in the Southwest made masks from leather, while the Cherokee used decorated **gourds**. These masks are used during storytelling.

Masks were treated as living things by the people who made them.

Did you know?

The Iroquois of the Northeast have a ceremony in which an ancient story is told. Members of the "False Face Society" put on masks and look for sick members of their community to heal. These painted wooden masks are considered to be sacred and living representations of spirits.

Ceremonies and rituals

All American Indian cultures have special ceremonies and rituals. These might involve dances, gatherings, and storytelling. Different groups show respect for different spirits or animals. For example, the owl and cougar are special to Cherokees in the Southeast because they are in their creation story. Many groups hold ceremonies to give thanks for the natural world around them.

Great New Moon Ceremony

In the Cherokee culture, the Great New Moon Ceremony was celebrated in the fall. The Cherokees believe the world was created at this time of year. People gathered to share food and dance. The celebration was a way to give thanks to their Creator. Some Cherokees still observe this festival today.

Sun Dance

The Sun Dance is a Sioux religious ceremony. During this ritual, men shed their blood to show thanks. They use sharp bones and sticks to pierce their upper body. Sun Dancers enter a **trance** and may have **visions**. This provides guidance for their tribe.

In 1883 the U.S. government outlawed Sun Dances, as well as a number of other American Indian religious practices. This decision was reversed in 1934. Today, Sun Dances are held on some Sioux reservations during the summer.

YOUNG PEOPLE

In the Blackfeet culture, young people use a vision quest to connect with the spirit world. They go to an isolated place, such as a mountain, and **fast**. This makes them weaker, and they may have a vision.

A vision quest helps young people discover their own personal animal spirit guide, which could be a bear, buffalo, coyote, wolf, or any other creature. Blackfeet believe this animal spirit helps the person throughout his or her life.

Rites of passage

A rite of passage is a sacred act performed to celebrate when a person moves from one life stage to another. Birth, becoming an adult, marriage, and death are all rites of passage. American Indians had rituals for many life changes, such as when a person became a leader. Some of these rituals are still continued today.

Names

Northern Plains Indian men used to get new names with each new life stage, to reflect their activities or personality. It is thought that the famous Lakota chief known as Sitting Bull was called Jumping Badger when he was born. After his first success in battle, his father gave him the name Sitting Bull. This had been the father's warrior name.

Sitting Bull helped his people gain victory against the U.S. Army at the Battle of the Little Bighorn in 1876.

Sunrise Dance

Western Apache girls mark the beginning of their womanhood with a Sunrise Dance. The girl's godmother dresses her for the ceremony. The community sings songs about the character Changing Woman from the Apache creation story. The girl dances to the songs, stepping gently from one foot to the other. This ritual gives her the physical and spiritual strength of Changing Woman. She also practices skills she will need as an adult.

This Apache girl is taking part in the Sunrise Dance. She is painted in sacred clay and cornmeal.

YOUNG PEOPLE

In American Indian hunter and warrior societies, manhood traditionally came after boys took part in a successful hunt or had their first experience in battle. Today, many young American Indian men serve in the armed forces to prove their manhood.

DAILY LIFE AND CUSTOMS

American Indians traditionally ate local plants and meat from animals they hunted. Acorn mush was a popular dish among American Indians in California. It took hours of work to grind the acorns and get rid of their bitter taste by soaking them in hot water.

Many American Indians described months and seasons according to what could be eaten at that time. They held festivals to celebrate important foods.

Green Corn Festival

The Green Corn Festival is a Pueblo tradition that continues today. "Green corn" is ripe and ready to eat. People celebrate a good harvest with dancing and feasting, and they give thanks to their creator. Green corn is delicious, but the Pueblo leave most cobs on the stalk so that it dries. They harvest the dried corn later and use it to make cornmeal, which they can eat all winter.

Did you know?

Eastern and Woodland Indians grew corn, squash, and beans. These three food crops were a very important part of their diet. They were called the "Three Sisters" by tribes such as the Iroquois and Wampanoag because they grew well together and were often eaten together in a dish called succotash.

These Navajo girls are demonstrating how corn is traditionally ground. They are using special stones called a *mano* and a *metate*.

Potlatch

Northwest Coast Indians have a giveaway ceremony called a potlatch. *Potlatch* comes from a word that means "to give." American Indian leaders need to show generosity to increase their status.

In a potlatch, the host serves more food than guests can finish. Salmon is the traditional food, along with berries, seaweed, and meat. After the feast, guests take leftovers and gifts home with them. The host might also give away blankets and other goods as gifts.

Storytelling

In the past, American Indians did not have books. They told stories instead. This was how history and culture were passed on from one generation to the next. All American Indian cultures have creation stories. These stories tell how Earth was formed and how the people came to live where they were. There are also stories that tell how animals came to be the way they are. In some, animals talk and act like people. Some of these tales have a message at the end and help teach children how to behave properly.

Joseph Bruchac (born 1942)

Joseph Bruchac is a storyteller and author. Some of his ancestors were Abenaki Indians in the Northeast, and much of his work reflects his American Indian roots. He has written books for both children and adults. He is also a professional storyteller, retelling the traditional stories of the northeastern Woodlands peoples.

Some stories were told only at certain times of the year. Storytellers had to learn their craft carefully, because stories had to be told the same way each time.

Cochiti storyteller dolls

The Cochiti are Pueblo Indians who live in New Mexico. Helen Cordero (1915–1994) was a Cochiti Indian who wanted to preserve her tribe's storytelling traditions and remember her storytelling grandfather. In 1964 she began sculpting clay figures of storytellers sharing traditional tales with children.

Today, many Cochiti potters produce storyteller dolls like these.

Toys

Many traditional American Indian toys and games helped children understand their own world and the sacred world. Some tribes played a ring and pin game, in which a ring or bundle of twigs is attached to a cord. This is thrown in the air and then caught on the pin. On the Southwest Coast, tribes such as the Zuni batted a shuttlecock made of corn and feathers with their hands. Many toys had religious importance.

Dolls

Many American Indian dolls help children learn about and respect their way of life. Some dolls are very simple. For example, Iroquois cornhusk dolls have no faces. This was to discourage vanity. The Iroquois believed that the corn spirit in the doll would choose which face to show the child.

These faceless cornhusk dolls are dressed in buckskin clothes.

The world's largest gathering of American Indians is a powwow that takes place every year in Albuquerque, New Mexico. In April 2011, more than 3,000 American Indian singers and dancers performed over three days to huge crowds.

YOUNG PEOPLE

Powwows are an opportunity for young people to explore and express their traditions and cultural heritage. Young singers and dancers perform and compete at powwows wearing the **regalia** of their individual tribes. Some regalia combines symbols in new ways. The ways children get involved in powwows today shows how American Indian cultures change with the times.

This young dancer is performing a grass dance in a competition.

Dance

American Indians dance to honor their cultures and ancestors—and each other. It is another way they express their identity as native peoples. Like storytelling, dancing is a way to pass traditions down from one generation to the next.

Young Hopi people take part in a Butterfly dance in late summer. They dance in pairs and are accompanied by singers. The girls wear colorful headdresses called *kopatsoki*, which are made by their partners. The dance is performed to ask for rain and a happy, healthy life.

The Tohono O'odham people in the Southeast dance to fiddle music. Their dances include a circle dance called a *kwariya*, which is performed by couples linked in a chain.

The hoop dance involves moving hoops that represent birds and butterflies.

Maria Tallchief (born 1925)

Maria Tallchief was born into a wealthy Osage family in 1925. She began studying ballet at the age of four. Her family moved from its reservation to Beverly Hills, California, so she could study with the best teachers. Maria performed her first solo dance at 15 and soon became a professional ballerina. She was the first American Indian prima ballerina, starring in ballets in the United States and Europe.

Animal dances

Many American Indian dances reflect the importance and movement of animals. The Ho-Chunk people of the Great Lakes have dances that show the flight of geese and swans. The Iroquois are famous for their buffalo and bear dances, while several Pueblo tribes in the Southeast perform deer dances.

Musical instruments

Rattles, flutes, and drums are the most important American Indian instruments. Instruments are made from wood, gourds, turtle shells, deer hooves, and other natural materials.

The Yaqui people of the Southwest perform deer songs. A deer dancer wears rattles on his legs and ankles and may also carry hand rattles made from gourds.

Drums

Northwest Coast peoples make beautifully painted drums that are hit with a beater. The paintings on the drums often show scenes from creation stories or important animals.

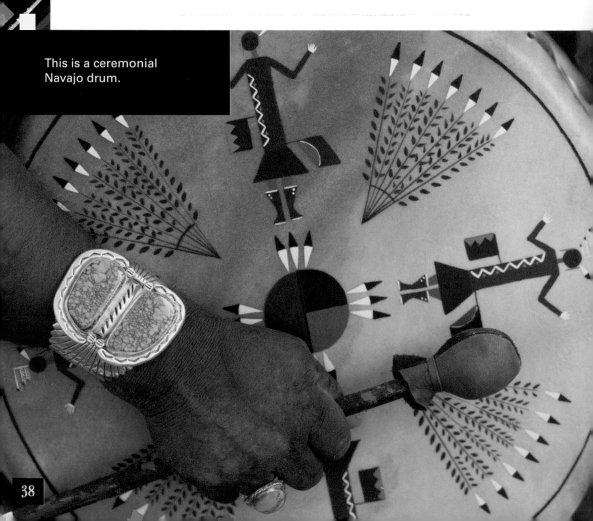

This is a ceremonial Navajo drum.

The Cochiti people of the Southwest make drums from sections of hollow tree trunks. Leather is laced around the two ends to produce a distinctive sound when struck.

The Iroquois people play water drums. Water is placed inside the wooden drum, and the drumskin is soaked to make it tighter. The water changes the sound that the drum makes.

Did you know?

Some tribes, such as the Kaw people of the southern Plains and the Chippewa in the North, have special drumkeepers. The keepers are responsible for the care of the drums. To them, drums are not just objects— they are also spiritual beings. To many American Indians, drumming represents the heartbeat of Mother Earth.

Singing

Like storytelling, singing is another way American Indians pass down their history. Singing is regarded as a form of prayer. For many American Indians, it is one of the most sacred forms of expression.

Stories are put into songs so that new generations can remember them correctly. Some songs, such as lullabies, are enjoyed as part of everyday life, while other songs are more religious. American Indians communicate with the spirit world and the Creator through singing.

Some songs are so sacred that they can only be sung by certain people at certain times. In other American Indian cultures, people have the right to sing certain songs, and they are also allowed to sell them to other singers.

AMERICAN INDIAN CULTURES IN THE 21ST CENTURY

There is no single American Indian culture. During the 1800s, the U.S. government tried to force American Indians to mix with the rest of the population. Many American Indians were ~~absolutely~~ forced to live on reservations, some of which were far from their traditional homeland. Many homelands contained precious resources that the government wanted. The government outlawed some of the Indians' religious practices, and it became difficult to follow traditional ways of life. American Indians were forced to adapt. Their various cultures today, like other modern cultures, are a mixture of past and present, growing and changing as they move into the future.

This Navajo man is making an intricate sand painting.

This museum display includes a large birchbark canoe.

Museums

Millions of objects from American Indians' past are preserved in museum collections. This gives people a chance to see everyday items such as moccasins and clothes, tools and weapons, jewelry, and other beautiful creations. Unfortunately, some of these objects were stolen from their rightful owners, and many American Indians were upset that their belongings were in museums. Today, some museums are changing the way they handle and display American Indians' cultural heritage. They invite American Indians to share their knowledge, so that the public can get a better understanding of traditional American Indian art and culture.

Through dance, art, storytelling, food, and pride in their heritage, American Indians of all cultures continue to express themselves, their people, and their place in the world today.

TIMELINE

BC

18,000–15,000 — Scientists believe the first American Indians arrive in North America from Siberia

AD

1492 — Christopher Columbus lands in the West Indies

1565 — Spanish colonists set up the first European settlement in present-day Florida

1620 — English colonists settle in Massachusetts and receive help from local tribes

1838 — Most southeastern tribes are forced to move to reservations. This journey is known as the Trail of Tears. Some Seminoles hide in swamplands to avoid being moved.

1870s–1880s — Plains Indians are forced to move to reservations

1887 — The Dawes Act divides up American Indian land, in an attempt to make the tribes adapt to white society

1887 — Pueblo potter Maria Montoya Martinez is born

1925 — Dancer Maria Tallchief is born

1942 — Writer and storyteller Joseph Bruchac is born

1960s — American Indian communities start to protest past wrongs and celebrate their cultures

1964 — Helen Cordero starts to make Cochiti dolls

1985 — Wilma Mankiller becomes the Cherokee Nation's first female principal chief

2004 — The National Museum of the American Indian opens in Washington, D.C.

CULTURAL MAP

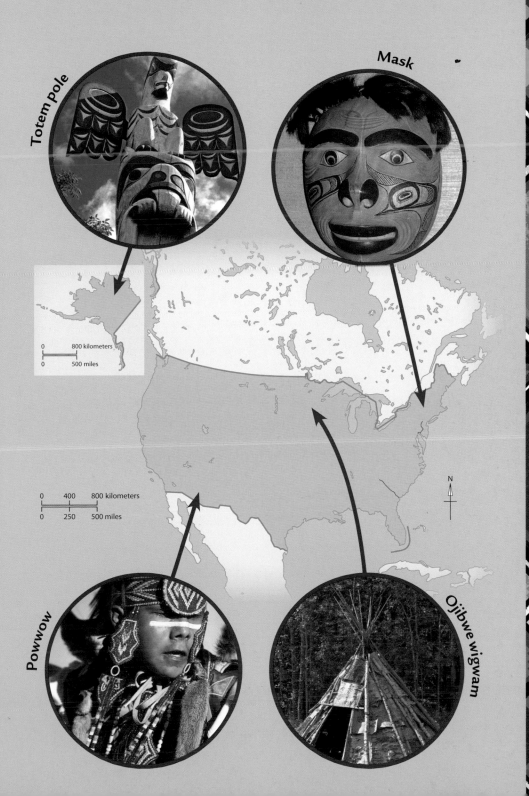

Totem pole

Mask

0   800 kilometers
0   500 miles

0   400   800 kilometers
0   250   500 miles

N

Powwow

Ojibwe wigwam

43

GLOSSARY

ancestor relative from a very long time ago, such as a great-great-grandparent

breechcloth strip of material worn between the legs and held up with a belt; also called a loincloth

clan group of families or villages that share a common culture

coup blow or strike. Some tribes counted coup, or the number of times a warrior touched an enemy during battle.

creation story story that explains how an American Indian culture began

culture customs, social organization, and achievements of a particular nation, people, or group

custom way things have been done for a long time

diplomat person skilled in keeping good relations between various individuals and groups

fast to go without food or drink for a certain period of time

game wild animals that are hunted for food

gourd large, fleshy fruit with a hard skin

heritage anything from the past handed down by tradition

lodge type of American Indian home lived in by extended families

nomad person who has no fixed home, who moves from one place to another for much of the year

regalia traditional clothing worn during ceremonies

reservation piece of land set aside by the U.S. government for American Indians, sometimes far away from the tribes' original homes

ritual formal actions in a ceremony

sacrifice when something, often a slaughtered animal, is offered to God

spiritual connected to religion and holy things

tan make animal skin into leather, usually by soaking it in a special substance such as a solution of oak bark

tipi cone-shaped tent made of animal hides or bark

tradition customs that are passed on from one generation to the next

trance partially conscious state, when a person does not respond to anyone or anything

umbilical cord cord that connects a baby to its mother before birth

vision kind of dream that holds meaning

Western countries and societies that are economically developed

FIND OUT MORE

Books

Bruchac, James and Joseph. *The Girl Who Helped Thunder and Other Native American Folktales*. New York: Sterling, 2008.

First Nations of North America series. Chicago: Heinemann Library, 2012.

Kissock, Heather. *American Indian Art and Culture* series. New York: Weigl, 2011.

Murdoch, David Hamilton. *North American Indian* (Eyewitness). New York: Dorling Kindersley, 2005.

Websites

www.josephbruchac.com
Visit this website to find out more about Joseph Bruchac's writing and storytelling.

Visit the following websites to find out more about some of the tribes mentioned in this book:
www.blackfeetnation.com
www.cherokee.org
www.choctawnation.com
www.havasupai-nsn.gov
www.kawnation.com
www.lumbeetribe.com
www.navajo-nsn.gov
www.sioux.org

Places to visit

Chippewa Valley Museum, Eau Claire, Wisconsin

www.cvmuseum.com

This museum has information about the Chippewa people.

The Indian Pueblo Cultural Center, Albuquerque, New Mexico

www.indianpueblo.org

Visit this cultural center to find out more about different
Pueblo Indian cultures.

Museum of the Cherokee Indian, Cherokee, North Carolina

www.cherokeemuseum.org

Visit this museum to find out more about Cherokee culture.

The Museum of the Red River, Idabel, Oklahoma

www.museumoftheredriver.org

Learn about the Choctaw and Caddo cultures at this museum.

The National Museum of the American Indian,
Washington, D.C.

www.nmai.si.edu

Visit this museum to find out about the many and varied
American Indian cultures.

More topics to research

What topic did you like reading about most in this book?
Did you find out anything that you thought was particularly
interesting? Choose a topic that you liked, such as food, art,
or religion, and try to find out more about it. You could visit
one of the places mentioned above, take a look at one of
the websites listed here, or visit your local library to do some
research. Topics to think about include Sitting Bull and the
Battle of the Little Big Horn (1876), the Dawes Act (1887), or
how to make a wigwam!

INDEX

ancestral lands 10, 21, 40

baskets 18
beadwork 16–17
blanket robes 18
body paint 16
Bruchac, Joseph 30
buffalo 7, 14

celebrations 5, 16, 25, 28, 34–35
ceremonies and rituals 7, 16, 21, 22, 23, 24–27, 29
clans 6
clothing 5, 14–15, 18
Cochiti storyteller dolls 31
corn 28, 29
coup sticks 7
creation stories 20, 21, 22, 24, 27, 30
culture: what it is 4

dance 5, 34, 35, 36–37, 38
dolls 32–33
drums 38–39

family and society 6–13
food 8, 28, 29, 34

Great New Moon Ceremony 25
Green Corn Festival 28

healers 7, 8, 23
homes 6, 8, 10, 12–13
horses 7

hunting 7, 10, 11, 14, 20

lacrosse 33
lodges 6, 22
longhouses 12

Mankiller, Wilma Pearl 9
Martinez, Maria Montoya 19
masks 22–23
men's roles 7
military service 27
moccasins 15, 16
moving 10
museum collections 41
music and instruments 38–39

names 26

ornament 14–19

pemmican 8
performance 34–39
places to visit 47
potlatch 29
pottery 19, 31
powwows 34–35

regalia 35
religious beliefs 7, 20–27, 32
reservations 4, 21, 25, 40
rites of passage 26, 27

singing 39
Sitting Bull 26

spirit world 21, 23, 25, 33, 39
storytelling 23, 24, 30–31, 39
Sun Dance 25
Sunrise Dance 27

Tallchief, Maria 37
tipis 12
tools and weapons 11
totem poles 22
toys and games 32–33
tribal groups 4, 6, 10

U.S. government 4, 40

warriors 7, 11, 16, 21, 33
weaving 14, 18
wigwams 13
women 8–9, 27

young people 17, 25, 27, 33, 35